All About Your

Contents

Intelligent, friendly, always ready to join in any activity. These are the characteristics which have helped make the Jack Russell Terrier one of the most popular breeds in Britain and the United States.

If you want to know more about its background and character, and how to choose, care for and train a Jack Russell, then this is the book for you.

But is the Jack Russell the right breed for you? Certainly its good points far outweight the bad, but you should consider both advantages and disadvantages very carefully.

The out-going Jack Russell thrives on family life.

THE POSITIVES
Size

A Jack Russell is a handy size for modern living. He stands around 14 inches at the shoulder – small enough to fit into an apartment. Yet there is nothing fragile or delicate about the breed.

Maintenance

Well-bred Jack Russells have few health problems and are generally easy to care for. The rough-coated variety need an occasional tidy, but this is neither difficult nor time-consuming.

Feeding and Exercise

The Jack Russell does not need a vast amount of food and thrives on a fairly basic diet. He will take as much exercise as you care to give him, but be equally happy sitting at your side if you want to stay at home.

Guarding

The Jack Russell is a friendly breed, more likely to lick an intruder than attack him! But he is very quick to sense the approach of strangers and will usually give a noisy warning.

THE NEGATIVES
Trainability

Quick to learn – sometimes too quick! The Jack Russell is very intelligent and can outsmart the average human most days. You will have to work very hard indeed on his training.

Small, and easy-to-care-for, this is a breed that adapts well to modern living.

Sociability

Well bred and well brought up Jack Russells are a delight to own, but early socialisation with other dogs is a must. The Jack Russell may come in a small package, but he thinks he's a much bigger dog, and unless his energies are channelled constructively, he will happily take on your neighbour's Rottweiler or Dobermann!

However, if you do train your Jack Russell properly and socialise him with other dogs, you will have a faithful companion who will be your loyal and fun-loving friend for many years to come.

Size And Shape

Jack Russells come in all shapes and sizes. Despite its popularity, the breed was only recognised by the English Kennel Club in 1990 (and had to wait until 1997 for the American Kennel Club to follow suit). Many unregistered dogs are called Jack Russells by their owners, but often these bear little resemblance to the correct type.

The traditional Jack Russell is quite a long-

DID YOU KNOW?

Among the famous artists who have painted the Jack Russell are Sir Edwin Landseer, Arthur Wardle and Maud Earl.

legged dog, with a harsh weatherproof coat that keeps him warm on a cold winter's day. He is mostly white, with the occasional black or tan patch, usually on his head, but sometimes on the body as well, and is a handy weight – around 16 lbs (7.25 kg) as an adult.

Life Expectancy

Jack Russells are a long-lived breed. Virtually all make double figures, many reach fourteen or fifteen years old, and quite a few are still happy and healthy well into the late teens. Buying a Jack Russell is a long-term commitment.

It is important to socialise your Jack Russell with other dogs.

What's In A Name?

Breeds are often named after the place they originally come from, like the Manchester Terrier, or they may be named after the job they do, such as a Retriever. Only a few bear the name of the person first connected with the breed. The Jack Russell Terrier is probably the best known of these. But just who was Jack Russell?

He was an English clergyman, in 19th century Devon. His passion was foxhunting, and he used his terriers to bolt foxes for the hounds to chase. His terriers were renowned for their character, their tenacity, and also for their good looks. At first they were known as Parson Russell's Fox Terriers, then as other people kept the same type, they were called Parson Jack Russell Terriers. Nowadays, most people just refer to the breed as the Jack Russell, but the full title is more correct.

The breed is named after an English clergyman – with a passion for hunting.

A Fox Terrier

The Jack Russell's job was to find a fox in his earth, then bark and nip, generally making life so uncomfortable that the fox would run out of his den, and take his chance with the hounds that were waiting above.

A Jack Russell was never meant to kill a fox. If he did, there would be no hunting, and the terrier would not be very popular. Every hunt had its own terriers, and they were bred with as much care as the Foxhounds.

Built on athletic working lines, the Jack Russell was bred to keep pace with huntsmen on horseback.

The Working Jack Russell

Many Jack Russells still work today. Some still bolt foxes. Others spend time ratting or rabbiting. Sometimes they act as gundogs, running through undergrowth to flush out gamebirds for a hunter with a gun. In the United States their quarry is more likely to be raccoon or groundhog, and wherever there is vermin to be controlled, there is sure to be a Jack Russell to do this work.

Some members of the breed are still used for working purposes.

Because the Jack Russell is so popular, you will have no problem in finding a puppy – but what sort of puppy? This is a breed where it really does pay to do your homework, and take your time, rather than just buying from the first litter you see advertised.

Simply because there is such a demand, uncaring and unscrupulous breeders know that they can sell puppies easily. A responsible breeder, with a good reputation, may have a waiting list, and will want to ask you some searching questions about your home and your family. Please don't resent this – the breeder is only concerned for the welfare of the puppy.

Go to a reputable breeder when looking for a puppy.

Just A Pet?

On making enquiries about buying a puppy, a breeder will often ask "Is it just for a pet?" as though this is a somewhat second-rate occupation for a Jack Russell. In fact, most breeders want their puppies to be first and foremost members of their new family, but they ask this question because a dog that is destined for the show ring must meet certain structural and cosmetic requirements. A Jack Russell that is too big or too heavily marked, for example, will not win prizes in the show ring, and a breeder will not want to see such a puppy competing at shows if it stands no chance of winning.

If your interest is in working your terrier, do buy a puppy from working stock. Any Jack Russell has the instinct to work, but doing it efficiently and legally is a different matter. It is likely that you will need more help and advice than your puppy, and this can only come from those that already have the experience.

Dog Or Bitch?

First-time owners are often advised that a bitch is easier, but that is not really the case. A male is often the better choice for a family as he will accept everyone equally, while bitches often give their allegiance to one person.

Coat/Colour

Jack Russells come in a variety of coat types, from smooth through to shaggy. Whatever the length of the coat, it should be harsh and straight, with a layer of dense, soft undercoat, which provides insulation and weatherproofing.

Coat type and markings will vary.

The Jack Russell is mainly white, but often has markings of black and/or tan. Ideally, these are confined to the head with just a small patch at the base of the tail.

Choosing A Jack Russell

An Older Dog

Should you buy a puppy? Puppies are tremendous fun and give great pleasure as they grow up into mature adults. However, for some people an older dog, which has already gone through the destructive and disobedient stages of growing up, is a more sensible choice. With a breed as popular as the Jack Russell, it is inevitable that some find themselves looking for new owners. In most cases, an adult Jack Russell will settle quickly into a new home.

More Than One

Two are twice as much fun, and Jack Russells can be very collectable. Never be tempted to take two puppies from the same litter, as they will be very difficult to train, getting into every bit of mischief possible, and thinking up a few tricks you never even considered. Never be tempted to have three Jack Russells. All terriers have the occasional argument and one against one will not usually cause too much of a problem. If three are together, the third one will join in with possibly disastrous results.

What To Look For

It makes no difference whether the pups have been reared in the house or in a kennel as long as they have been well looked after and properly socialised. Unless you already know of a breeder who has Jack Russell Terriers, ask your national Kennel Club for advice as to the whereabouts of puppies. It is still possible to buy a Jack Russell that is not KC-registered, but there is no guarantee that the puppies from unregistered parents will be typical of the breed in terms of size and appearance.

A Healthy Puppy

Always try to see the puppies with their mother so you can watch how they react with each other. The mother should have a good temperament and be happy to show off her puppies to you. Avoid a shy, nervous puppy that cowers in a corner. Jack Russell puppies are normally very bold and curious and will come rushing to play with anyone or anything new.

Ears – clean and fresh-smelling.

Anus – clean, no evidence of soiling.

Behaviour – bold and curious.

Eyes – bright and clear.

Nose – free from discharge.

Mouth – check for any soreness on the gums.

Abdomen – well-covered but not swollen, which could indicate worm infestation.

Jack Russell puppies are great escape artists. Youngsters will chew, dig, and wriggle through the smallest of gaps. It is impossible to make the whole house puppy-proof, so concentrate on making allocated areas completely safe.

Indoor Crates

Probably the most useful piece of equipment that you can buy for your new Jack Russell puppy is a wire crate. If you buy one that is big enough for an adult (about 24 ins by 18 ins and about 18 ins high), it will last for years. The crate provides a safe 'den' for the puppy when he wants to rest, it can be used to transport him safely in the car, and the puppy can be safely confined when he is not supervised. Obviously he must not be shut in for long periods, but, used sensibly, the crate is of great value both for the puppy and his owner.

Beds And Bedding

Jack Russell puppies chew. Virtually any bed will be destroyed, so, at first, place a strong cardboard carton inside the crate and line it with soft, easily washable bedding. As the puppy grows, the box can readily be replaced with a slightly bigger one.

Feeding Bowls

Your Jack Russell needs his own bowls for food and drinking water. They should be heavy and easy to clean. Stainless steel is ideal. Ceramic bowls look attractive, but can be broken.

Toys

Puppies often enjoy cheap and easily replaceable toys more than the very expensive ones. An old sock, twisted into a nice firm knot, will provide hours of fun. Any toys will be chewed, and homemade ones can easily be replaced when they become too worn. Remember, a small puppy's teeth can be every effective so it is essential to ensure that all toys are 100 per cent safe.

Toys have more value when they are not left around all the time. Make sure that you are the one in possession of the toy at the end of a play period. Jack Russell puppies can become possessive, and must never be allowed to guard their toys from others.

Collar And Lead

A lightweight collar and lead is suitable for a puppy.

Once your puppy starts to go out he will need a collar and lead, and a tag with your address on it. Don't forget that puppies grow rapidly and you will have to replace the collar as your pup gets bigger.

Identification

A collar can get broken, or even be deliberately removed if your puppy is lost. You may consider having your puppy injected with a tiny microchip, which carries a unique number that can be read by a special scanner. Many vets now offer this service.

The New Arrival

Try to collect your new puppy fairly early in the morning. This will give him the whole day to explore his new surroundings, and he will be more likely to settle when evening comes.

Introducing The Family

Everyone will want to meet the new arrival, and this can be frightening for a puppy. Let him make friends in his own time with the family – but try to keep the neighbours away for a day or two. Children will want to cuddle him and play with him, but they must be taught to respect his needs. Puppies are very like small children. They will play hard and then fall asleep quite suddenly. That is the time to pop your puppy in his crate and shut the door so he can rest quietly andprivately.

Settling In

The crate will be very important to a puppy in his first few days, and, when he goes in there, he must be allowed to rest. It is a good idea, at first, to restrict him to just a small area of the house, especially when he is unsupervised.

Give your puppy a chance to explore.

The puppy's breeder should provide a diet sheet, and ideally, a sample of the food that he is used to. It is a big trauma for a little puppy to go to a new home, and a change in diet will be sure to cause an upset tummy. Your puppy may be reluctant to eat at first, but there is no need to panic – and never try to tempt him with lots of different food. If your puppy ignores his food, just quietly remove it, and try again later when he has had a good sleep. Jack Russells are keen on their food, and your pup will soon be clearing his plate.

The new arrival will miss the company of his littermates to begin with.

The First Night

When it is time to go to bed, your Jack Russell might well feel lonely, and cry pitifully. This is when it is an advantage to have a crate. Make sure the bed is warm and comfortable and that the puppy has been out to relieve himself. Put him to bed with a biscuit, turn off the light and leave him. He will soon settle down.

With tactful handling, your puppy will soon settle.

Feeding Your Jack Russell

Complete, complementary, canned, flake, meat and biscuit – the choices are bewildering. Traditionally, dogs were fed on a meat and biscuit diet. Nowadays most people choose to feed a complete food, which has been carefully formulated to include all the nutrients that a dog needs. Do not buy a premium quality puppy food for your Jack Russell puppy – the protein level is too high.

Mealtimes

When your new puppy first arrives, he will need four small meals each day. Allow him to eat as much as he wants, then remove any that is left.

By the time your Jack Russell is three months old, he will still be eating about the same amount, but it can now be split into three slightly larger meals. Between four and six months he will become less interested in his midday meal, and you can naturally wean him on to just two meals each day. This is also the time to start changing from a puppy food to an adult formula. Never introduce a new type of food when your Jack Russell is facing any sort of stressful situation – such as vaccination, worming or teething.

A Jack Russell will be fully grown by the time he is around nine months, and by then he should be eating a

Select a diet that is low in protein.

16

regular adult food. Again, you must choose a diet that is fairly low in protein. High levels of protein can cause both skin and behavioural problems in Jack Russells. It is a matter of choice whether you feed once or twice a day during adult life.

Special Diets

Jack Russells can be greedy, and some do have a tendency to put on weight! Special diets are available for obese dogs, and these are also suited to elderly, less active ones as well. Your veterinary surgeon should be able to advise you about the most suitable diet for your pet at any stage in his development.

The veteran Jack Russell may require a specially formulated diet to meet his needs.

Bones And Chews

Chewing is all part of growing up – and if you don't want gnawed furniture, give an alternative.

Hide chews are dangerous for Jack Russells. This is a breed with such strong teeth and jaws that hide chews can easily be destroyed. If pieces are swallowed, they cannot be digested and will cause a dangerous obstruction.

The best chew toys are strong nylon ones, which, although not completely indestructible, will give a Jack Russell hours of fun.

Regular grooming enables you to keep a check on your Jack Russell's general health.

Daily Routine

Jack Russells do not need extensive grooming, but it is a good idea to accustom your terrier to regular brushing. It also gives you an opportunity to check your dog over on a regular basis.

A dog that lives outdoors, in a kennel, will shed its coat twice a year, but those living in centrally-heated houses are likely to lose their hair more gradually. Brushing encourages loose hairs to come out and massages the skin.

Whether your Jack Russell is rough-or smooth-coated, he will have a harsh topcoat and a shorter, softer undercoat. A slicker brush will remove any dead hair, preventing it from being deposited all round the house!

No matter how careful you are, your Jack Russell may occasionally pick up fleas. There are a variety of preventative measures that you can take, so it is best to ask your vet for advice.

Twice a year, a heavy-coated dog will need stripping out completely. A grooming parlour will do this, but it is not difficult to carry out the

A heavy-coated dog ready for stripping.

task yourself. When the hair is ready, it will come out quite easily if you give a few hairs a little pull. Start near the tail, and work methodically towards the head. It takes some time to completely strip a dog, so it is best to do it over several short sessions.

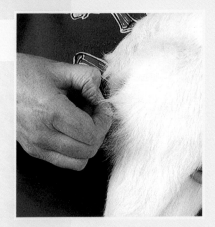

Stripping the coat is done using finger and thumb.

Nails

A Jack Russell that gets plenty of exercise on hard surfaces is unlikely to ever need his nails cutting, but if they do get too long, there are a variety of nail-clippers on the market. Ask your vet to show you how to do this, as it is important not to cut into the quick of the nail which will cause bleeding.

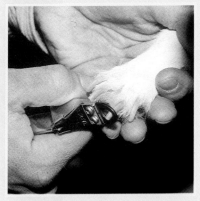

Ask an expert how to show you how to trim nails.

Teeth

If you feed a complete diet and also provide chewy toys, your Jack Russell's teeth will stay shining white. If they do start to get stained, use a special dog toothpaste to clean them. If tartar is allowed to accumulate on the teeth, they will need to be scaled by your vet.

Regular brushing will keep teeth and gums healthy.

Training Your Jack Russell

Training starts the moment your new puppy arrives home. Be consistent in your training, giving praise and rewards when your puppy gets it right rather than punishing bad behaviour.

DID YOU KNOW?

Parson Jack Russell was a great friend of the Prince of Wales (later King Edward VII). At the age of 78, Russell danced in the New Year with the Princess of Wales, at Sandringham House.

DID YOU KNOW?

One of the best known Jack Russells is Wishbone, who has his own TV show in the United States. Wishbone's AKC registered name is Willowall Soccer.

Your Jack Russell must learn to respect all members of the family.

House Rules

Puppies are rather like small children. They respond best to firmness and kindness. If you are consistent, they soon understand what is acceptable.

If you don't want your puppy to sleep on the sofa, then never allow him on it. You cannot expect him to understand if he is allowed to do something one day, then punished for the same action the next day.

House Training

Take the puppy outdoors frequently, and especially after meals or a play session, and when he has just woken up. Always go to the same spot and use the same phrase, such as "Hurry up" or "Be quick". As soon as he does perform, give the puppy lots of praise so he knows that he has pleased you.

If he does make a mistake around the house, don't draw attention to it, and never scold him. Instead, quickly clear it away, and use a deodorising spray to mask the scent.

It is important that your dog learns what is allowed – and what is considered undesirable behaviour.

Training Your Jack Russell

Basic Commands

Probably the first word any puppy learns is "No!". "Sit", "Stay" and "Come" take a little bit longer, but even a very young puppy will soon learn what is meant.

Sit

Teach your Jack Russell to sit by holding a small tidbit of food (cheese is popular) over his head, so that he has to sit down to get to it. As the dog goes into the Sit position, give the command, and reward him with lots of praise. Eventually you can start saying "Sit" before you offer the treat, and soon you will be able to dispense with it altogether – although you should use an occasional reward to remind your puppy.

Use a treat to teach the Sit.

Come

Teaching your puppy to come is easy – you will be amazed how quickly a Jack Russell puppy will learn his name and come racing towards you when you call him. Reward this response with the occasional tidbit and you will soon have built up a strong foundation for a recall.

The Recall presents few problems!

Down

"Down" is probably the most important command your puppy can learn, as a dog that will drop to order will be under control at all times. Once your Jack Russell has learned the Sit, lower the tidbit towards the floor to encourage him into a Down position.

Remember to keep the training sessions very short, and always end on a positive note.

Lower the treat towards the ground, and this will encourage the dog to go into the Down position.

Lead Training

Although your Jack Russell puppy will not be able to go out into public places until he has finished his vaccination course (see Page 30), you can teach him how to walk on a lead in the garden. Start by putting his collar on – something he may not like at first! The best method is to fasten the collar, then distract the puppy with a game or a tidbit, and he will soon forget all about it.

The next step is to attach the lead, and follow your puppy where he wants to go. After a little while, ask him to follow you, giving him lots of praise and encouragement.

The Outside World

Socialisation

Once your puppy has completed his vaccination programme, he can go out into

the big wide world. Puppy playgroups are organised in many areas, and these provide socialisation and basic training for youngsters. It is essential that any puppy gets used to other people and other animals from an early age. This is doubly important for a breed like the Jack Russell, which is very full of its own importance. A small Jack Russell puppy can get into serious trouble if he has not learned to accept other breeds.

From around five or six months of age, you should consider taking your Jack Russell to dog training classes. In both the UK and the USA, the national Kennel Club runs a Good Citizen scheme for dogs and their owners where a basic standard of training is achieved over a period of weeks. This should be within the reach of every Jack Russell Terrier.

A Jack Russell hates to be left out of family activities.

Places To Go

Jack Russells are always full of fun, and hate to be left out of family activities. Most adore travelling in the car, and it is important to establish a safe routine. A terrier-sized crate will fit in most cars that have a tail-gate, and a puppy that has been crate-trained within the home will accept this very readily. There are two important points to remember with regard to car travel:

• Never leave your dog loose in a car while you are driving. If there is not enough room for a crate, buy a specially designed harness which can be attached to the regular seat belt.
• Never leave your Jack Russell in a car on a sunny day. The sun's rays will soon make the interior of the vehicle unbearable, and your dog will literally be cooked to death.

DID YOU KNOW?

When the World Cup soccer trophy was stolen in 1966, it was found under a bush by a Jack Russell.

Exercising Your Jack Russell

The Jack Russell is an energetic breed, and even small puppies like to be on the go most of the time. However, puppies do need quite a lot of sleep. Do not take a small puppy for long walks – a game in the garden is quite sufficient.

Resist the temptation of over-exercising your puppy.

When the puppy is a little older, and you want to go out walking together, take time to build up the distance slowly. Just like an athlete, a dog needs to build up his fitness over a period of time. When a Jack Russell is fully matured (at about eighteen months of age) he will, if fully fit, be able to walk as far as you can!

On Lead

Lead exercise is very valuable for building up fitness, and a Jack Russell that is regularly walked on hard surfaces will

have strong pads and short nails. Sometimes it is essential for your dog to be kept on a lead. No dog, however well-trained, should be allowed to walk along a road off-lead. A terrier can be easily distracted by a cat or another dog, for example, and could easily cause an accident by chasing across the road in front of a car.

Free Running

Whilst controlled exercise on a lead will help to build up your Jack Russell's fitness, all dogs need the opportunity to run freely. A Jack Russell can get all the exercise he needs in a good-sized garden, especially if you are playing with him. Many Jack Russells enjoy a game of football, and will retrieve toys, but do be careful that these are safe. A ball that is too small can become stuck in the throat, while a pointed stick can cause serious damage to a dog's eye or mouth.

Swimming

If you are lucky enough to live near the sea, a lake, or a safe stretch of river, your Jack Russell will soon become a competent swimmer. Most dogs are natural swimmers, and it is one of the best forms of exercise that your dog can have. However, do make sure that your dog does not swim in a place where there are strong currents.

DID YOU KNOW?

John Russell was born on December 21, 1795 and died on April 28, 1883. More than 1000 people attended his funeral.

A free run in a safe area is a source of huge enjoyment.

Mini Agility

This is a sport that might have been invented just for Jack Russells. It does need a dog (and a handler) with a high standard of fitness, and agility training should not start until the dog is around twelve months of age.

Introduce your dog to the agility obstacles one by one.

With careful training, your Jack Russell will soon become confident.

Playing Games

The Jack Russell is so intelligent that unless he is exercised mentally, as well as physically, he can become bored. Boredom leads to other problems; destructive behaviour and even aggression can be symptoms of a dog needing more stimulation.

A Jack Russell is quick to learn new tricks, and enjoys showing off. By working together you will establish a firm bond with your dog, and have a well-behaved and faithful friend.

Obedience Training

All Jack Russells should receive basic obedience training. If you enjoy working with your terrier in this way, you may consider continuing with the classes, and aiming for a higher standard. At the highest levels, Competitive Obedience requires a degree of precision that is completely alien to a quick-witted Jack Russell, but the breed can, and does, compete very successfully in the lower classes.

Health Care

Jack Russells are a healthy, hardy breed, and suffer few health problems. However, it is essential that you keep up-to-date with both vaccination and worming programmes.

Vaccinations

All puppies must be vaccinated to protect them against several potentially fatal diseases. These are : - Distemper, Infectious hepatitis, Parvovirus, Leptospirosis and Rabies (excluding Britain).

   The exact timing of the vaccinations depends on the particular vaccine used, and your vet will advise you. Most involve a first injection at any time from eight weeks of age, with a second at twelve weeks. Your Jack Russell will need a regular booster injection each year.

Worming

Your puppy should have been wormed by the breeder, and it is advisable to continue with a regular worming programme throughout your Jack Russell's life.

Roundworm

Puppies are usually infected with roundworm from their mother. Very rarely, roundworm can cause problems if ingested by children, and in extreme cases can affect their eyesight, so it is essential that all dogs are wormed regularly throughout their life.

Tapeworm

Occasionally a dog may be infested with tapeworm. This long, flat worm lives within the intestine, with its head firmly anchored. Rice-like segments break off from the end of the worm, and can be seen in the faeces, or, more commonly, stuck to the hair around the dog's anal region.

Heartworm

This parasite lives in the heart and can cause significant problems. The intermediate host is the mosquito and so dogs living in tropical areas are more likely to be affected. If you live in an area where heartworm is endemic, it is essential to adopt a worming programme.

Important note: Veterinary worming preparations are very effective and simple to use, so there is no reason not to use them on a regular basis for routine prevention.

Breed Specific Conditions

Lens luxation, a painful eye condition, has been seen very occasionally in Jack Russells, and breeders are encouraged to have their dogs tested to check that they are clear. When buying a puppy, it is advisable to check that both parents have been tested.